THE
STORM
BREAKER

PERSONAL BOOKLET

DAILY READINGS: SELWYN HUGHES
GROUP ICEBREAKERS
AND DISCUSSION QUESTIONS:
IAN SEWTER

Published 2012 by CWR, Waverley Abbey House, Waverley Lane, Farnham, Surrey GU9 8EP, UK. CWR is a Registered Charity – Number 294387 and a Limited Company registered in England – Registration Number 1990308.

Bible-reading notes included in this booklet previously published by CWR in *Every Day with Jesus – The Stormbreaker*, March/April 2012. Group icebreakers previously published in *Every Day with Jesus* March/April 2012 and the free online resource EDWJextra, March/April 2012 and May/June 2012.

For a list of National Distributors visit www.cwr.org.uk/distributors

All Scripture references are from the Holy Bible: New International Version (NIV), copyright © 1973, 1978, 1984 by the International Bible Society.

Song extract on page 5: Adm. by worshiptogether.com songs excl. UK & Europe, adm. by kingswaysongs.com tym@kingsway.co.uk

Concept development, editing, design and production by CWR

Cover image: CWR

Printed in England by Bishops Printers

ISBN: 978-1-85345-838-5

CONTENTS

A WORD OF INTRODUCTION

WELCOME TO *THE STORMBREAKER* DVD resource. The sessions which follow are based on an issue of *Every Day with Jesus* written by Selwyn Hughes, which focused on a storm that raged many, many years ago. Selwyn was exploring those three momentous days when Jesus faced the worst the world could throw at Him, yet overcame. And because He overcame, the cross and resurrection provide 'anchor points' which today, can hold us fast amidst life's storms.

Different countries, cultures and communities have their own Easter customs – from dousing each other with water to flying kites; from egg rolling to egg hunting and eating! Yet amidst the frenetic activity, and even with a packed programme of church events, I fear that I have become too familiar with the Easter story itself, that awe-inspiring moment when eternity broke into time. It was so much more than a one-off event in history – its effects reverberate today and will do so forever. The cross of Jesus is more than just a place of peace and refuge; Christ endured the cross that we might truly *live*.

This series focuses entirely on the cross, and my prayer for us all as we reflect on the theme is best summed up in the words of this song:

May I never lose the wonder, the wonder of the cross.
May I see it like the first time, standing as a sinner lost.
Undone by mercy and left speechless watching
wide-eyed at the cost,
May I never lose the wonder, the wonder of the cross.[1]

May we never lose the wonder of the cross.
Sincerely yours, in His name

Mick Brooks
Consulting Editor

1. Vicky Beeching, extract from 'The Wonder of the Cross', copyright © 2007 Thankyou Music.
   See copyright page for further details.

FOR GROUP LEADERS

HOW TO USE

This resource is designed to include all you need for five small-group sessions. It comprises five DVD sessions, icebreakers, group discussion questions and prayers based on each DVD session, and Bible readings to be used between each session.

PREPARATION

1. Watch the week's DVD session before the meeting.

2. Select the questions you think will be most useful for your group to look at. You may want to use them all, depending on the time you have available. We suggest you plan for 30–45 minutes.

THE SESSION

1. From Session 2 onwards you could start each session by reviewing how the group found the daily readings of the previous week. What did they learn? Do they have questions to raise? How did God speak?

2. Play the DVD and go straight into the icebreaker question, which is designed to get people chatting.

3. Use the questions you have selected.

4. Move from discussion into prayer. There is a prayer included in the material that you could use at the end.

5. Encourage the group to use the daily readings in the days between sessions. The readings expand and build on the topics covered in the DVD, and introduce some new themes. If the group members are not used to daily Bible reading, encourage them to develop this habit. If the group members are already in a routine of Bible reading and prayer each day, you might want to discuss how best to work these new readings into their time.

6. On the last session – Session 5 – you might suggest meeting once more after the last week's reading to pray and consider the whole experience together.

SECURE IN G

ICEBREAKERS
• Describe your feelings about someone who has shown you love and care – a parent, friend, relation, spouse, teacher etc.

• How did you first become aware of God's love for you?

FOR GROUP DISCUSSION
• How well do you cope in the face of difficult circumstances?

• Why may problems prove or disprove our theological convictions?

- What do people try to cling to when faced with problems?

- Why may the historic message of the cross be relevant to those caught in a storm today?

- Why is death a beginning as well as an ending?

- How can the cross be an anchor point to overcome doubt?

- Consider how God the Father received His Son into heaven. (See Acts 2:32–36)

PRAYER

Father God, when we find ourselves amidst the storms of life and are tempted to doubt Your care for us, may we cling to the cross of Your Son Jesus, our Saviour, the ultimate expression of Your love. Amen.

GOD'S GREATEST WORD

FOR READING AND MEDITATION – JOHN 3:1–16

'For God so loved the world that he gave
his one and only Son ...' (v.16)

LET US CONSIDER the fact of God's love and its importance to mature Christian living. Many years ago, I sat down to prepare a sermon on the theme of God's love. I began to go through the Bible book by book in order to find references on the theme. You can imagine my surprise when I discovered that the first four books of the Bible have no mention of God's love at all, though of course it is quite clear from the passages that God really does love everybody. I relaxed when I came to Deuteronomy (what someone once called 'The John of the Pentateuch'), for in this book there are several references to God's eternal love. The same is true of many of the other Old Testament books.

However, when I read through the first three Gospels I was again surprised – there are no clear references to God loving us in Matthew, Mark or Luke. There is an incidental reference to God's love in Luke 6:32–36, but no clear or direct statement. Once again, of course, it is evident from these three books also that God loves us, yet the statement is not directly made.

Then I came to John's Gospel and read in our text for today the first New Testament declaration of God's love. It was like a burst of sunlight in the darkness, and it simply overwhelmed my soul. The great preacher C.H. Spurgeon once said that if all of the Bible was lost to us and we had one text – John 3:16 – there is enough divine revelation in this one verse to present the gospel to the whole world. Let the words of this mighty text lie on your heart and mind as you travel through this day.

Gracious Father, it is as if Your heart is uncovered in these matchless words of John 3:16. Help me meditate on them throughout this day. I would put my heart up against Your heart, feel its beat and catch its rhythm. In Jesus' name. Amen.

THE MOTIVE BEHIND CALVARY

FOR READING AND MEDITATION – JOHN 3:16–21

**'For God so loved the world that he gave
his one and only Son ...' (v.16)**

I MAKE NO apology for holding you to John 3:16 for one more day. Believe me, you will be all the better for it. There is more of the gospel packed into these 26 words than in all other literature. I have been preaching on this verse, and expounding it in my writings, for over 40 years, and I feel like saying as did the Queen of Sheba concerning Solomon's Temple: 'The half was not told.'

Tennyson's lines about the flower in the crannied wall come to mind as I reflect once more on what has been called 'This text of texts':

*If I could understand
What you are, root and all, and all in all,
I should know what God and man is.*

But how does this verse relate to our theme of the cross and resurrection? Well, the glory of the cross is shown in the motive that lies behind it. And here is that motive – 'God so *loved* ...' When you see that the cross is not the cause of God's love, but that God's love is the cause of the cross, then it takes on a new and glorious perspective. God does not love us because Jesus died, but Jesus died because God loved us. We must not leave out the little word 'for', because it links the verse with the preceding one. It must be read like this: 'The Son of Man must be lifted up ... for God so loved the world.' God loved us so much that He gave up His only Son for us. But for the love of God, this lifting up would never have taken place.

O God, I see and feel that this verse is charged with the new wine of the kingdom. Just to sip it makes me feel intoxicated – with redemption. But help me not to sip of it; help me to drink deep draughts of it. In Jesus' name. Amen.

YOU WANT PROOF?

FOR READING AND MEDITATION – GALATIANS 2:11–21

'... the Son of God ... loved me and gave himself for me.' (v.20)

HAVING SPENT A couple of days looking at the categorical statement concerning God's love contained in John 3:16, we ask ourselves this question: why, in the light of such a clear unfolding of the divine love, should we ever find ourselves doubting it? Perhaps it is because, when lashed by the gales of doubt, our souls cry for something more than a verbal revelation of love; we need something vital. We hunger for *proof.*

One of my favourite forms of study is to read the lives of the 'saints'. In biblical terms, of course, everyone who has a personal relationship with Christ is considered to be a saint. Over the centuries, though, theologians have endowed only a few outstanding Christians with this title – Saint Augustine, Saint Bernard, Saint Teresa, and so on. What has interested me when reading about the lives of these remarkable Christians is that although the way in which they came to the awareness of God's love differs, the place of revelation was always the cross. And no wonder! For there the heart of God is unveiled.

St Teresa, for example, went one day into her private oratory, where she noticed a picture of Jesus being scourged. She had seen it a hundred times before, but in a moment of blinding revelation she saw it as she had *never* seen it before. One of her biographers says of her: 'She saw God suffering – suffering for love and suffering for her. It struck her to her knees, sobbing in pain and wonder, and when she arose, she arose a new soul.' Those who would doubt the love of God need only to draw close to Calvary. There the revelation is more than verbal. It is vital. Here is the *proof.*

O God, bring me again to the cross so that I might see Love. Hold my sin-dulled gaze there until, in its blinding revelation, I see still more of its length and breadth and depth and height. In Jesus' name I ask it. Amen.

LIGHT IN THE DARKNESS

FOR READING AND MEDITATION – GENESIS 15:1–19

'When the sun had set ... a smoking brazier with a blazing
torch appeared and passed between the pieces.' (v.17)

I KNOW OF no Old Testament story that illuminates the theme we are pursuing – finding an anchor point in the cross whenever our hearts are assailed by doubt – better than this.

Abraham, or Abram as he was known at this time, found God's promise that his descendants would be as numerous as the stars somewhat staggering – but nevertheless he believed. Then came promise number two: 'All this land will be yours.' This was not as easy to accept so he asks for some reassurance. It is as if Abraham is saying: 'God, I can believe your first promise, but on this second one I need a little help.' And a little help is given. Abraham is instructed to take some animals and birds, cut them in half (excepting the birds), and arrange the halves opposite each other. After he has done this, he falls into a deep sleep and is engulfed by a great darkness. Suddenly, Abraham sees a smoking brazier and a blazing torch passing between the carcasses. What did they mean? The invisible God had drawn near to confirm His previous promise and seal His covenant. He was saying in effect: 'May what has happened to these animals happen also to Me if I do not uphold My word' (see Jer. 34:18).

What has all this got to do with the cross? Well, whenever like Abraham you are engulfed in the darkness of doubt, and God seems very far away, remember that the hands that carried the fire pot and blazing torch 2,000 years earlier, and brought light into his darkness, are the hands that were crucified for you. Stand in awe before the tree and let all your doubts and hesitancies be extinguished in the flame of Calvary's love.

O God, though You have a thousand ways of reassuring me that Your promises are true and that I am the object of Your love, no way captures my heart more than the cross. I shall be eternally grateful. Amen.

HOW DID YOU FEEL, GOD?

FOR READING AND MEDITATION – ROMANS 8:28–39

'He who did not spare his own Son,
but gave him up for us all ...' (v.32)

WE SPEND ONE more day reflecting on the truth that the cross provides us with a firm anchor point whenever we find ourselves doubting that we are loved by God.

A minister tells of taking his little girl to school for her first day there. She seemed to be free of any concern as they drove along, but when they pulled up at the school gates she became silent for a while, and then with trembling lips said: 'Daddy, I don't want to get out.' The minister says he fought a Herculean urge to say, 'OK, let's forget it and go home', but he knew that was not the way. 'Darling,' he said, 'I'll go in with you and stay around for a little while.' Of course, once she was in the classroom curiosity took over, and she soon forgot that he was there. As the father walked back to his car, the verse I have chosen for today came into his mind, and reflecting upon it he prayed this prayer: 'Is this how You felt God? Is what I feel now anything like what You felt when you gave up Your Son?' If so, he concluded, then it explains so much: the proclamation of the angels, for example, to the shepherds at Bethlehem – a proud Father announcing the birth of His Son. It explains the voice at Jesus' baptism: 'You have represented Me to absolute perfection.' And it explains how His heart must have felt when the Saviour cried: 'Father, take this cup away.'

How God felt about His Son going to the cross we can only conjecture, but this we know for sure – He gave Him up for you and me. What an anchor point this gives us when assailed by doubts concerning the Father's compassion and mercy. He gave His best for us, says the apostle Paul, *we need not doubt His love.*

Father, the cross is living proof that You care. Help me cast my anchor at its firm foundations. Throwing out the anchor is something that by an act of will I must do. You provide the anchorage, I must avail myself of its security. Amen.

SECURE IN G

ICEBREAKER
• List the attributes of a perfect parent.

FOR GROUP DISCUSSION
• How can a cosmic God be interested in you as one of six billion people on an insignificant planet in a minor galaxy?

• Why may we feel that we are insignificant to God?

• In the book *When Bad Things Happen to Good People*, Rabbi Kushner presents the view that God is good and loves His creation but is less than omnipotent. Why is this view popular but incorrect?

• Discuss the concept of God as Father.

• Why should God think about us and plan for our future?

• How might a wedding ring be likened to 'graven hands'?

• C.S. Lewis concluded that we humans are big enough to ask the great questions of the universe but not big enough to understand the answers. Could agnostics and atheists regard this statement as a 'cop out'?

PRAYER

Lord of life, thank You that You are big enough to know about the tiniest details of our lives. When storms come, help me to know that I can bring every concern to You, confident that You care deeply. Amen.

STOICISM IS NOT THE WAY

FOR READING AND MEDITATION – 1 CORINTHIANS 12:12–26

'If one part suffers, every part suffers with it ...' (v.26)

WE TURN OUR attention now to another anchor point which the cross provides – a secure ledge on which our anchors can fasten when our lives are lashed by the strong winds of unmerited sorrow and suffering.

Such times come to us all. I once heard of an American financier, a multi-millionaire, before whom the strongest of men quailed. His frown could cow the most ferocious, and his eye was awful in anger. Yet when his wife died (his first wife) after no more than six months of marriage, this hard man became distraught and cried out for comfort. Sooner or later, everyone faces the need for comfort and consolation. When that hour comes, where will we turn? Christians turn to the cross, or perhaps more correctly, the Christ of the cross. I make no apology, therefore, for turning your gaze once again in the direction of Calvary, but before we do, let's glance at some of the answers which the world puts forward in relation to this problem of unmerited sorrow and suffering.

The Stoics – those who believe you must stand up to whatever comes without allowing yourself to feel pleasure or pain – claim that their way is the only one that can get you safely through life. Their ideas are summed up by the poet Whitman (1819–1892), who said: 'Under the bludgeoning of chance ... my head is bloody but unbowed.' It is a noble attitude – noble, but very lacking. The Stoics feared that unless you shut out love and pity, the world of grief and sorrow would troop in behind. But if you are a harsh, insensitive person, you are an inadequate person. So although many in today's world try to live by this philosophy, this is not the way to meet unmerited sorrow and suffering.

Father, I see that steeling myself against life is not the way. I become less of a person by so doing. I want to respond to whatever comes in the way Your Son responded to it. Teach me that art. For His dear name's sake. Amen.

THREE WORLD-VIEWS

FOR READING AND MEDITATION – JOHN 6:60–71

'Lord, to whom shall we go? You have the words of eternal life.' (v.68)

TODAY WE ASK ourselves: what do some other religions believe about unmerited sorrow and suffering? First we come to Buddhism. Its philosophy is this: in life each of us will face sorrow and suffering. I would hold to this view as well. The Buddhist solution, however, is not the one which Jesus offers us. Buddhists believe that the way to be free of sorrow and suffering is to cut the root of desire, even for life, and to enter a detached, passionless state called Nirvana – a state of true happiness.

Then there is Hinduism. Hindus believe that there is no such thing as unmerited sorrow and suffering. Whatever is, is just. If you are suffering now, it is because you have done something wrong in a previous existence; what you are experiencing you have brought about by your own actions. A Hindu said to a missionary, 'Jesus must have been a terrible sinner in a previous life because He suffered so terribly in this one.'

When we consider the Muslim faith, we find the general approach is this – whatever happens is the will of God, and we must accept it as the will of God. On the surface, the message looks like the Christian one, but when you scratch the surface, you find that Muslims believe both good and evil are the will of God. All the good and all the evil are His will, and we must accept it.

There is a way to meet unmerited sorrow and suffering which, I believe, surpasses all these philosophies. It is the way of Jesus. Following His path doesn't take away the sadness and pain, but it does enable us to hold fast through the storm and emerge from it not shattered, but stronger.

Lord Jesus, thank You for providing a way for me through sorrow and suffering. Only by anchoring myself to Your cross will I find security. So I say with Simon Peter, 'Lord to whom shall we go? You have the words of eternal life.' Amen.

WHY JESUS CAME

FOR READING AND MEDITATION – JOHN 12:20–36

**'Now is the time for judgment on this world; now the
prince of this world will be driven out.' (v.31)**

TODAY WE ASK ourselves: how did Jesus view the problem of
unmerited sorrow and suffering? His attitude is so different from
others' that it strikes us with surprise.

Jesus accepted the fact of human suffering, and neither explained
it nor explained it away. If He attempted to explain it, His message
would merely have been another philosophy, for a philosophy has
to have an explanation for everything. Jesus' purpose in coming to
this world was not primarily to explain things, but to spell out the
'good news' – that in Him we can find life and power which enables
us to overcome all obstacles. The gospel may not explain, but it most
certainly brings about a change – a change of heart and a change
of mind. Jesus transforms suffering by using it, and shows us that
victims can become victors, tests can be turned into testimonies.

In an evangelistic meeting, I once heard a preacher say: 'If you
come to Christ you will never have any more problems.' I thought of
the early Christians who were in constant trouble, and reflected also
on the many Christians I knew who were going through the most
heartbreaking situations. It is not right to say to a non-Christian: 'If you
come to Jesus you will never have any more problems.' But it is right to
say: 'If you come to Christ you will find new strength to overcome your
problems.' Sometimes (not always) people who become Christians
have more problems to face than they had before – just because they
are Christians! Personally, I would rather face all kinds of problems
providing I have Jesus than have no problems and be without Him.

**Father, I'll have to change my vocabulary, for quietly I am changing my
attitudes. The things I thought might be stumbling blocks I am now seeing as
stepping stones. Difficulties are really doors. How wonderful. Teach me more.
Amen.**

WATCH THE LIGHTS!

FOR READING AND MEDITATION – MATTHEW 5:33–48

'He causes his sun to rise on the evil and the good, and
sends rain on the righteous and the unrighteous.' (v.45)

HAVE YOU EVER thought what would happen if, when a person became a Christian, he or she never had to face sorrow or suffering again? What would happen to the universe? It would soon become chaotic and undependable. If a Christian leant too far over a parapet, the law of gravity would be suspended, but if a non-Christian leant too far over, he would fall. In the real world, the law of gravity is not going to ask if a man or woman is a Christian or not; it goes to work irrespective of these considerations. The world is a hard school, and it helps to know the rules.

Again, take this example: suppose Christians were kept from getting knocked over by a car whenever they rushed into a busy street. What would happen? Christians would become champion jaywalkers, and would probably vegetate as a result. And why? They would lose the quickness of decision which comes from coping with a world of changing circumstances. I know, and you know, that when we cross a traffic-infested street, if we don't belong to the quick, we will soon belong to the dead! I will never forget what a policeman told me when I was a little boy living in the city of Birmingham. As I ignored the traffic lights and rushed across the road, he said 'Son, if you want to live long, keep your eye on the lights.' It was good advice and I have never forgotten it.

The New Testament does not teach that because we are Christians we will be exempt from sorrow and suffering. It teaches, however, that God will be in the sorrow and suffering to enable us to turn it to good account. Everything furthers those who follow Christ.

Father, I know it makes sense, but I confess there is still something in me that would wish to avoid all sorrow and suffering. There is a lesson I need to learn here. Help me not to miss it. Amen.

CAN GOD HEAL?

FOR READING AND MEDITATION – JAMES 5:7–20

'Is any one of you sick? He should call the elders of the church ...' (v.14)

WHILE MEDITATING ON this matter of sorrow and suffering, it is necessary to say a word about the suffering that comes from sickness or disease. Physical suffering is not what I had in mind when using the phrase 'sorrow and suffering' (I was thinking more of difficult and despairing circumstances). However, as there will be those of you reading this who believe in miraculous healing, I feel it might be helpful if I were to pause here to share my thinking on this issue.

God can and does intervene to deliver us from physical sickness and suffering, but it is more the exception than the rule. Not everyone who asks for healing gets healed; that is a simple empirical fact. Does this mean we ought to forget the whole business of praying for people who are sick? No, for we cannot measure the results of our prayers only by what we see. There may be no apparent or immediate physical changes, but who can measure the spiritual changes that come from prayer?

However much we cannot understand about why God allowed sorrow and suffering to enter His universe, this we can understand – He bears such suffering Himself. A God who does this can have my heart without any reservations whatsoever. Unlike the gods of other religions, who are distant and unapproachable, our God, in Jesus, came among us and felt all the disappointment, suffering and pain that we feel. As we walk through life and experience its pains, we can know that our God sympathises with us. And not only that. He is walking alongside us, ready not just to listen to our troubles but to enter into them with us, giving us the strength to continue and even to see good come about where we thought there was no hope.

O Father, give me a balanced view on this perplexing subject of healing. Help me see that all prayer is answered. You say, 'Yes', 'No,' 'Wait,' or 'Here's something different.' Teach me how to accept Your answer. In Jesus' name. Amen.

SECURE IN T

ICEBREAKER

• Discuss your experience of learning to drive and taking the test (or other relevant learning experience involving correcting failures).

FOR GROUP DISCUSSION

• Discuss the attitude of Thomas Edison and if you should be more like him!

• Why should we be careful about our 'self-talk'?

• What is Jesus' attitude to us when we fail? (See John 8:1–11)

FACE OF FAILURE

• How may others regard us? (See Luke 7:36–50)

• Try to find (on the internet), and then read and discuss the portrait of Jesus entitled 'One Solitary Life'.

• What lessons have you learnt from failure?

• How can eternal hope overcome temporary failure?

• Should every Christian be an optimist?

PRAYER

Jesus, please help us to see this issue of failure in a whole new light – help us not to 'beat ourselves up' when things go wrong, but to learn from our experiences. Take away our fear of failure as we trust You to order our next steps in life. Amen.

ALL CAN FALL

FOR READING AND MEDITATION – PSALM 130:1–8

'But with you there is forgiveness; therefore you are feared.' (v.4)

THERE IS ANOTHER anchor point we find at Calvary – the fact that when through our foolishness and pride we fall into sin, forgiveness is to be found at the cross. What an anchor point this is to secure the hull of our hearts after the enticements of evil have led us into some defiance of the divine commands. All of us stumble and fall into sin at times. Some of us crash. And when I say 'all' I mean 'all'.

On one occasion, when preaching in a church I used to pastor, I made the statement I have just made above: 'All of us stumble and fall into sin at times.' One of the elders came to me in the pastor's room following the close of the service and urged me never to use that same phrase again. 'There are some of us in this church,' he said, 'who haven't sinned in years, and we find it an affront when you give others the impression we might have fallen into sin.' I felt deeply sorry for the man because it was obvious to me (and many others) that there were clear evidences of pride at work in his life of which seemingly he was unaware. In the course of the conversation that followed, I was able, gently, to share how and where pride surfaced in his life. After this, I fully expected him to offer his resignation and walk out of the room, but he came towards me, flung his arms around me and wept on my shoulder for what must have been a full half hour.

So I say again; *all of us stumble and fall into sin at times.* Sometimes others may not know about it, sometimes (if it is attitudinal) we may not know about it. But always – God knows about it. That is why, as the old saying goes, it does not behove the best of us to look askance at the worst of us.

O God, help me face as this man did the truth that unacknowledged sins may be lurking in my heart. It is only in Your light that I can see light. I draw near to You so that I might be fully cleansed and made fully whole. In Jesus' name. Amen.

THE LAW OF LOVE

FOR READING AND MEDITATION – JOHN 13:31–38

**'Love one another. As I have loved you, so
you must love one another.' (v.34)**

I INVITE YOU now to consider the following statement: 'There is only one sin – the sin of making ourselves God – all the rest are sins.' I think that what the person who said that meant was this: the sin from which all other sins devolve is the sin of self-centredness. And not just self-centredness in itself, for throughout the ages even non-Christian philosophers have condemned self-centredness as being detrimental to effective living. The real sin is that by being self-centred we keep God out of the part He reserves for Himself – the centre of our being.

One of my concerns with contemporary Christianity is that we define sin too narrowly. We look for things that are obvious (such as adultery, stealing, lying etc), and then, because we do not see those things at work in our lives, say to ourselves: 'I am free from sin.'

Regular readers of *Every Day with Jesus* will be aware of my belief that the purpose of living is to reflect the ethos of the Trinity in the way that each one relates to the others in glorious other-centredness. This is a category of living which we don't hear much about in our churches, but it is pinpointed very clearly for us in the text before us today. Would you say that whenever we resist the law of love, which Jesus identifies so clearly for us in this scripture, we are committing sin? I would. We might shun the obvious sins, but then go on to violate the law of love with impunity. When I look at my life and think of it in terms of the broad categories of sin I have mentioned, there is not much that is wrong. But when I see how very often I fail to love as I am loved, my heart is ashamed – and I have to repent.

Lord Jesus Christ, You who modelled what it is like to love as You were loved, teach me to do the same. And when I fail, help me recognise my failure and lean upon You in deeper dependency. For Your own dear name's sake. Amen.

SELF-DECEPTION

FOR READING AND MEDITATION – 2 SAMUEL 12:1–10

'Then Nathan said to David, "You are the man!"' (v.7)

THE THOUGHTS OF the past few days may be considered by some to be making more of sin than salvation. I am aware of that danger and will do all I can to maintain a proper balance between the two. The reason I am exposing the subtle nature of sin is that we might more wonderfully enjoy the completeness of God's salvation, particularly the joy of a full and free forgiveness. My concern is that we might know just what kind of sins go on in our hearts so that we can bring them out, repent of them and experience the gift of God's forgiveness.

How easy it is to deceive ourselves that there is no sin in our being when there is. It is not hard to understand how this happens. A defence mechanism called 'denial' goes to work to help us ward off any discomfort or anxiety in our soul, and we go deeper and deeper into deception. This is what happened to David in the story we are looking at today. His sin, of course, was not subtle, but blatant and obvious. He coveted the wife of one of his captains and, while the army was in the field fighting battles, he seduced her. Then, fearing exposure, he contrived the death of her husband and added murder to treachery and lust.

If the 'man after God's own heart' could allow himself to be so self-deceived about such obvious sins as adultery and murder, how careful we ought to be about the more subtle sins of self-centredness, independence and pride. Self-deception is dangerous. It can keep us feeling spiritual, while at the same time choking the life out of our soul. God forbid that we become so self-deceived that God has to send a Nathan into our lives to point us out, mark us down and say: 'You are the man!' 'You are the woman!'

O God, if I am self-deceived, help me I pray, for I want to be free of everything that would rob me of Your presence and power. Time is short, and living for You is too precious to have it hindered by sin. Make me completely whole. Amen.

WHAT BECAME OF SIN?

FOR READING AND MEDITATION – PSALM 51:1–19

'For I know my transgressions, and my sin is always before me.' (v.3)

THE ISSUES WITH which we must first come to grips if we are to understand the message of divine forgiveness are these: we must not be content to define sin in broad categories (it can be subtle as well as obvious), and we must never minimise it.

It is the reluctance to face up to the gravity of sin which has led to the omission of the word from contemporary literature. Karl Menninger, a well-known American psychiatrist, in his book *Whatever Became of Sin?*, drew the attention of his peers to the fact that in today's world 'one misses any mention of "sin". It was a word once in everyone's mind, but it is now rarely if ever heard. Does that mean,' he asks, 'that no sin is involved in our troubles ...? Has no one committed any sins? Where indeed did sin go? What became of it?' He goes on to look at some of the reasons for the disappearance of the word 'sin', and points out that things which we used to call sin, and were dealt with by the church through confession and forgiveness, have now become crimes and are handled by the world. Other sins have been redefined in terms of sicknesses, or at least as symptoms of sickness, so that in their case, punishment is replaced by treatment. A third convenient device, called 'collective irresponsibility', has enabled us to transfer the blame for errant behaviour from ourselves as individuals to society as a whole.

To ignore the reality of sin is dishonest. To tamper with the labels and call a serious thing by a light name is very dangerous. We don't make a deadly thing innocuous by giving it a different name. Poison is still poison – no matter what other label we give it.

O God my Father, I see the folly of minimising sin. Give me a balanced sensitivity to this whole issue so that I might see the seriousness of sin and thus enter more joyously into the freedom of forgiveness. In Jesus' name. Amen.

ACCEPT WITH GRATITUDE

FOR READING AND MEDITATION – LUKE 7:36–50

'Therefore, I tell you, her many sins have been
forgiven – for she loved much.' (v.47)

WE HAVE TALKED a good deal about sin over the past few days;
now let us focus on forgiveness.

That God forgives us through the blood of the cross, is one of the
greatest themes in all the world, but it is still a mystery nevertheless.
Life that is built on the atonement, on the wonder of the fact that
despite the enormity and gravity of our sin God has found a way to
forgive us, is life indeed.

The reason why I have focused on the fact of sin over the past few
days is to prepare you (as far as I possibly can) to receive an even
greater revelation and appreciation of the wonder of forgiveness.
Through the sacrificial offering of Jesus on the cross, God has built
into the bedrock of the universe an anchor point for all those who
through their own choice find themselves engulfed in sin. We confess
our sins and then, as John puts it: '… he is faithful and just and will
forgive us our sins …' (1 John 1:9).

This does not mean, though, that because God forgives, you can
sin with impunity. A minister tells how one day a man came into his
church and told him that although he was a Christian, he had taken
to drink and became an alcoholic. As the minister prayed with him,
he began to sob and said, 'I know I'm in the gutter. But oh! … I don't
belong there, do I?' The minister put his arm around him and said,
'No, you don't belong there; you belong to God.' Remember that the
next time you fall into sin. *You don't belong there. You belong to God.*
Hurry always to the cross with your sins, and pray not only for pardon
but also for power – the power not to make the same mistake again.

**O God, I feel sad that so often I take Your forgiveness for granted, rather than
accepting it with gratitude. Help me see just what I have been saved from and
saved to – and come to an even greater appreciation of my salvation. Amen.**

ICEBREAKER

• What favourite song or hymn would you like played at your
  funeral?

FOR GROUP DISCUSSION

• Why may a Christian have no fear of death?

a) Why may the funeral of a Christian be a place of joy as well as
   sorrow?

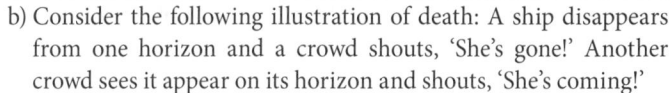

ST THE FEAR OF DEATH

b) Consider the following illustration of death: A ship disappears from one horizon and a crowd shouts, 'She's gone!' Another crowd sees it appear on its horizon and shouts, 'She's coming!'

• How did David view death? (See 2 Samuel 12:15–23)

• How could we convince others that the resurrection was a historical fact?

• Discuss the phrase, 'Because He didn't stay dead, you and I will not stay dead.'

• How may we encourage one another? (See 1 Thessalonians 4:13–18)

PRAYER

*Lord Jesus, thank You for Your
resurrection life, which You share
with all those who know and love
You. Please give us opportunities and
boldness to share the resurrection story
with others. For Your glory. Amen.*

DEVIL DEFIERS

FOR READING AND MEDITATION – REVELATION 12:1-17
'They overcame him by the blood of the Lamb ...' (v.11)

NOW WE LOOK at yet another anchor point the Easter message gives us – a solid rock from which to withstand the lies of the devil. So whenever you feel that you are being battered in this way, lashed by the winds of spiritual oppression, learn to do what I have been advocating through the whole of these studies – drop your anchor at the cross. Calvary spells defeat for the devil, and although he may not wish to acknowledge it, you must point him to it – if necessary, again and again and again.

In the passage before us today, five names are given to our spiritual adversary: 'the dragon', 'the serpent', 'Satan', 'devil' and 'the accuser'. 'The dragon' carries with it the thought of monstrosity – something ill-formed and unlike anything human. In the word 'serpent' there is the idea of cunning, slyness, and craftiness. The name 'Satan' implies opposition – an evil adversary. 'Devil' means deceiver and slanderer. 'The accuser' carries the thought of someone who makes lying accusations.

This gives you some idea of the force and personality that is against us when we come over on to the side of Jesus Christ. However, look at the weapons we have to fight with – they are threefold: the blood of the Lamb, the testimony of those to whom the blood has been applied, and the sacrificial spirit which carries them even unto death. Although we will never be able to avoid the attacks of the devil, through Christ and His triumph on the cross we are well able to withstand them. Make no mistake about it, the devil is a *defeated* foe. God knows it, the devil knows it, but all that is to no avail unless *you* know it.

Yes Father, I do know it, but I want to know more of it. Teach me how to stand against the wiles of the devil, and may I come through these next few days understanding more of the resources that are available to me in Christ. Amen.

KNOWING THE ENEMY

FOR READING AND MEDITATION – 1 JOHN 3:1–10

'The reason the Son of God appeared was
to destroy the devil's work.' (v.8)

WE SHALL LOOK a little later at how to withstand the wiles of the devil (and pick up on the points we raised yesterday), but first we must 'know our enemy'. Our text for today tells us that the reason Jesus came was 'to destroy the devil's work'. This raises the question: what sort of work is the devil engaged in? Let's look at the devil's *modus operandi* in detail.

One of the first works of the devil mentioned in Scripture was to call into question the fact of a revelation from God. God had said to Adam, 'When you eat of it you will surely die' (Gen. 2:17). The devil appeared on the scene and asked, 'Did God really say …?' (Gen. 3:1). The same devil who asked that question is at work in the world today, calling into question the fact of a revelation from God. 'How can you be sure the Bible is true and is from God?' he asks. Another aspect of his work is to deny the truth of God's revelation. When the devil found he could not get Eve to deny the fact that God had spoken, he suggested that what God had said was not true. 'You will not surely die' (Gen. 3:4).

A third aspect of the devil's work is to cast doubt on the benevolence of God: 'God knows that when you eat ... your eyes will be opened, and you will be like God, knowing good and evil' (Gen. 3:4). The cunning insinuation behind this remark was this: 'God is trying to keep something from you that is for your good; there is more to know.' Surely the devil has come to you with similar thoughts. But knowing where they come from is your security. Doubt is our adversary's chief weapon, and trust in God our biggest defence.

O Father, I see how important it is that I know something of how the devil works. Help me to trust You even in the face of massive doubt. Remind me at such times that there is a safe and sure anchor point at the cross. In Jesus' name I pray. Amen.

MORE OF THE SATANIC PLOY

FOR READING AND MEDITATION – JAMES 1:1–18

'... each one is tempted when, by his own evil desire,
he is dragged away and enticed.' (v.14)

WE CONTINUE UNCOVERING the way that the devil works in human lives. Bringing about the fall of Adam and Eve was one of Satan's greatest achievements, and it should not surprise us that he uses similar deception, accusations and other strategies still.

A further device of Satan, which he employed with Adam and Eve, was to appeal to their physical, aesthetic and intellectual nature. '... the fruit of the tree was good for food' (an appeal to the physical being); 'pleasing to the eye' (an appeal to the aesthetic being); 'desirable for gaining wisdom' (an appeal to the intellectual being) (Gen. 3:6). It is through these three avenues that Satan achieves some of his greatest conquests. And note: he tempts us through the things we like, not the things we don't like.

Take first the physical. How many people are ruined daily by pushing them towards physical indulgence in the area of food and drink? Then there is the aesthetic. God has created us with an appreciation for the aesthetic but, before we know it, Satan pushes us to become preoccupied with it. He continues until, without realising it, the 'beautiful' things have taken over our lives and have driven out all thoughts of God. Third, the intellectual. Sometimes people who could not be lured into sin through the physical or the aesthetic are brought there through the desire to gain wisdom and knowledge. They become brilliant in mind, but use their brilliance to argue God out of existence. If the devil can induce us to accept any sort of light – intellectual light, scientific light, philosophic light – instead of the light that comes from Calvary, he has us in his grip. He has repeated the victory which he accomplished at Eden.

My Father and my God, thank You for reminding me how the devil approaches me through the things I like rather than the things I don't like. Keep me ever alert to the satanic ploy and ever close to Your heart. In Jesus' name. Amen.

THE POWER OF THE BLOOD

FOR READING AND MEDITATION – REVELATION 1:4–19

**'To him who loves us and has freed us from
our sins by his blood ...' (v.5)**

NOW THAT WE have looked at some of the ways in which Satan works, the next question is: how do we overcome him?

We overcome him in the same way that the people in the book of Revelation overcame him – through the blood of the Lamb. Every accusation Satan levels at us must be met by the blood of Christ. If Satan comes to you and says, 'You are a guilty sinner and deserve everlasting punishment', all you need do is point to the blood that was shed for you on Calvary and the accuser cannot say another word. He is immediately silenced. This is the argument which prevails against the devil whenever he approaches God and tells the truth about you. If it is a lie that he used before God then you don't have to bother about that, for God sees through his lies. It is the truth that hurts – the truth that you are a sinner and worthy of death. Or the truth, perhaps, that because you have failed you deserve to be banished for ever from God's presence. But remember also the truth of God's Word: 'If we confess our sins, he is faithful and just and will forgive us our sins and purify us from all unrighteousness' (1 John 1:9).

Martin Luther, it is said, had regular visits from the devil. He declared: 'The devil came to me and whispered, "You are a sinner and you are lost for ever."' 'Not so fast,' retorted Martin Luther, 'you told the truth when you said I am a sinner, but you lied when you said I am lost for ever. I am a sinner trusting in the Lord Jesus Christ and therefore I am saved.' We are lost, that is true, but the truth that we are saved by the blood of Christ must always be set against it.

Gracious and forgiving God, I rest not in my own righteousness but in Yours. Through the blood of the cross I am saved – and saved for all eternity. How can I ever thank You sufficiently? All honour and glory be unto Your name for ever. Amen.

CHRIST *WITHIN*

FOR READING AND MEDITATION – COLOSSIANS 1:24–29

' ... the glorious riches of this mystery, which is
Christ in you, the hope of glory.' (v.27)

EVEN A CASUAL reader of the New Testament could not help but notice that the letters of the apostle Paul are punctuated with dozens of references to the defeat of the devil. At the cross, Paul tells us, Jesus disarmed and triumphed over the devil, and all the principalities and powers at his command. First-century Christians had no difficulty believing this; why do we have so much difficulty in believing it today? 'But we do believe it,' I hear you say. Then why, I ask, do you allow the devil to have so much room and influence in your life? It is one thing to believe that Jesus has defeated the devil; it is another thing to live in the glow, the wonder and the *reality* of it.

I know many Christians who hold a good theory concerning Satan's downfall at the cross, but don't seem to know how to move across from theory to experience. Let A.W. Tozer tell us how. 'The secret of overcoming the devil is to hang on to the fact that Christ is in you, the hope of glory. I'm not foolish enough to say I am not afraid of the devil. He has got some judo holds I have never heard of. But he can't handle the one to whom I'm joined; he can't handle the one to whom I'm united; he can't handle the one whose nature dwells in my nature.' Ah, there's the secret – being in Christ and having Christ in you. It's a mystery, of course, as Paul points out, but it is a mystery which can be experienced even though not fully comprehended.

William Law (John Wesley's one-time teacher) said, 'A Christ not in us, is a Christ not ours.' A Christ above us is not enough. A Christ beside us is not enough. A Christ ahead of us is not enough. Only a Christ within us is enough.

O Father, help me see that I have all I need to combat the wiles of Satan when I have You within. May I walk through this day and every day in the sure knowledge that the One who conquered Satan now lives in me. Amen.

SECURE IN T

ICEBREAKER
• What has most impacted you from our studies in this issue, and how will you change as a result?

FOR GROUP DISCUSSION
• Consider the statement of Oswald Chambers, 'Life is more tragic than orderly.'

• What 'kingdoms' and institutions have been shaken in your lifetime?

THIRD DAY

- Consider Professor Henry Drummond's words, 'If you seek first the kingdom of God and His righteousness, you will still have to face problems; but if you don't seek first the kingdom of God then you will have nothing but problems.'

- How can we avoid being overwhelmed by the storms of life? (See Luke 8:22–25)

- If you feel able to, share about a storm you have been through and how God helped you in it.

• What anchors our soul? (See Hebrews 6:13–20)

PRAYER

Heavenly Father, please anchor these eternal truths in our hearts so that, with You, we may ride the storms of life. Thank You that nothing can shake the kingdom you have established – and we are part of it! Amen.

TRUTH PREVAILS

FOR READING AND MEDITATION – 2 CORINTHIANS 13:1–10

'For we cannot do anything against the
truth, but only for the truth.' (v.8)

TODAY WE ASK the question: how far can evil go in a world of this kind? It can go so far and no further. It can crucify the Creator of the universe on a cross. That is a very long way. It can do that today, it can do it tomorrow, but the third day – No! For goodness rises from the dead, and goodness has the last word. We read that the guards who were watching the tomb of Jesus were like 'dead men', while at the same time Jesus was resplendently alive. Evil went a long way on that first Easter, but it only went two days. The third day God raised His Son from the dead.

One of the elements of evil is lies. This poses another question: how far can lies go in this universe? Well, lies were one of the things that put Jesus on the cross. Lies took the truthful Son of God and pinned Him to a tree. Three days later, however, the lies were overcome by truth. The universe is not built for the success of a lie.

I read that the Tamils of South India – people I just love being amongst – say, 'The length of the best concocted lie is just eight days.' They mean that in eight days a lie goes to pieces – broken by the very nature of a moral universe. When the diminutive Joseph Goebbels was propaganda minister for the Nazis during World War II, the Germans used to say, 'Lies have short legs!' Lies may seem good in the short run, but they are bad in the long run. A lie, you see, has nothing behind it but itself. The universe makes a lie break upon the universe.

So how far can lies go? A long way, some might say, but really not very far. They can go the first day, the second day, but the third day – No!

O God, what confidence this gives me to know that nothing can work successfully against the truth. May my life bear witness to that truth, today and every day that I remain here on the earth. In Jesus' name I pray. Amen.

'THE TERRIBLE MEEK'

FOR READING AND MEDITATION – MATTHEW 5:1–12

'Blessed are the meek, for they will inherit the earth.' (v.5)

WE CONTINUE MAKING the point that the Easter story gives us the solid assurance that force, evil and lies can go so far but no further.

In the play *The Terrible Meek* by Charles Rann Kennedy, one of the soldiers at the crucifixion speaks to Mary the mother of Jesus in these words: 'I tell you, woman, this dead Son of yours, disfigured, shunned, spat upon, has built a kingdom this day that can never die. The living glory of him rules it. The earth is *his* and he made it. He … has been moulding and making it through the long ages. Something has happened up here on this hill today to shake all our kingdoms of blood and fear to the dust. The terrible meek, the fierce agonising meek, are about to enter into their inheritance.' People cried for Jesus' blood at the scene of the crucifixion, but they went away beating their breasts (Luke 23:48), knowing this was a place to repent, not rejoice. The smiters smote themselves and were eventually laid in a tomb, just as Jesus was laid in a tomb. However, He arose – and they did not. They are buried in oblivion; He goes marching on.

The last word in human affairs is not lies, not violence, not force, not intimidation, not fear, but love. If you feel overwhelmed by what you read in the newspapers or see on television, as evil men and women seem to get away with so much, keep in mind that they are now in the first and second day. A third day is coming when evil will be swept from the universe and the kingdom of God is ushered in. Today meekness might seem like weakness, but it will not be long now before the meek, *the terrible meek*, will enter into their inheritance.

Loving heavenly Father, forgive me for my impatience, yet when I see 'truth on the scaffold and wrong on the throne' I want to do something about it today. But teach me how to have patience with the patience of God. In Jesus' name. Amen.

JESUS IS KING – NOW!

FOR READING AND MEDITATION – HEBREWS 2:1–9

'But we see Jesus ... now crowned with glory and honour ...' (v.9)

ONE OF THE great missionary hymns begins, 'Jesus shall reign where'er the sun doth his successive journeys run ...' Bold words in these dark days when the authority of Christ is so widely denied. Of course Isaac Watts, the hymn writer, was looking forward to a time when the rule of Christ would be unchallenged by the whole universe, but we must also see that the New Testament teaches us Jesus reigns now.

The writers of the epistles (Paul and Peter particularly) emphasise the fact that the kingship of Christ is not something to be established in the future, about which they ought to speculate, but something in the present they could enjoy. This truth is best brought out by the writer to the Hebrews, who says in our text for today: 'But we see Jesus ... *now* crowned with glory and honour' (my emphasis). Note: '*We see*,' not 'we *shall* see.' It was not the faint hope that one day Jesus would occupy the throne that sustained and inspired the early Christians in their struggle against the evil forces and lies of their day, but the sure knowledge that Christ was on the throne then – crowned, glorified and triumphant.

You and I, in the midst of the difficult days through which the world is passing, need a similar assurance. We too need to see that Jesus reigns in the midst of world confusion, and that what is happening is allowed by Him to happen. Why He allows it to happen is beyond our comprehension, except that the bottom line with God is that He knows exactly what He is doing. Just as He was in charge of events when His Son lay in the darkness of the grave, so He is in charge of events now. Reason may not believe it, but faith most surely does.

O God, help me hold on to this truth, that You are not struggling to make Your way to the throne – You are there now. And crowned with glory and honour. In the face of all that might contradict this truth – I believe. Amen.

HALF-GODS ARE NO GODS

FOR READING AND MEDITATION – MATTHEW 6:28–34

'But seek first his kingdom and his righteousness ...' (v.33)

I DO NOT consider myself to be a prophet in the predictive sense, but I feel 'the spirit of prophecy' upon me as I write. It seems clear to me that we are living in a of political and national unrest. Nations are being shaken before our very eyes. Totalitarianism, Fascism, Naziism, Communism have broken down or are breaking down. Here and there they raise their heads, but they have the stamp of death upon them. Fascism made the state supreme, Naziism made the race supreme, Communism made the ordinary people supreme. All these systems are half-gods and hence no gods.

A minister tells how a few years after World War II, he spoke to some prominent German leaders on the text before us today. As he described the loving totalitarianism that characterises Christ's kingdom, they pounded their fists on the seats in front of them. Afterwards, he asked why they had done that. They said, 'You seemed to sense why we turned to Naziism. Life for us was at a loose end – compartmentalised. We needed something to bring life back into wholeness, into total meaning and goal. We thought Naziism could bring that wholeness. But it let us down, let us down in blood and ruin. Now we see that what we were seeking for was the kingdom of God. We chose the wrong totalitarianism.'

I suspect that behind the various revolts that we are witnessing all over the world – the revolts of youth, races, nations – men and women are seeking for the kingdom of God and don't know it. What I think we are witnessing in our day is the shaking of earthly kingdoms in order that the unshakeable kingdom might appear.

Father, can it be that what I am witnessing in the earth are the birth pangs of a new order? Are you about to usher in the fullness of Your kingdom? Make me prayerful, expectant, ready and spiritually alert. Even so, come Lord Jesus. Amen.

DON'T GO ON APPEARANCES

FOR READING AND MEDITATION – ROMANS 8:18–27

'... we ... groan inwardly as we wait eagerly for our adoption
as sons, the redemption of our bodies.' (v.23)

THE QUESTION WE began with a few days ago, and to which we now return, is this: What are we to do when we feel overwhelmed by the evil that seems to be mounting in our world? How do we stay calm and secure in an age that seems to be half-crazed, if not entirely mad?

Once again, we must drop our anchor in the Easter revelation and remind ourselves that because of what happened there, all will be put right on the third day. The moral universe will not bend to evil. It may appear to do so, but if the cross and resurrection teach us anything, they teach us that appearances must be treated with suspicion. Good Friday appeared to have crushed the life out of the Son of God, but Easter Sunday saw Him step forth in all the power of a resurrected life. Good Friday appeared to bring an end to the miraculous ministry of the Man from Galilee, but Easter Sunday saw Him demonstrate the miracle of miracles – rising from the dead. If Easter means anything, it means that God always has the last word. Men might appear to have it today, but all we need to do is to wait until tomorrow, or the day after tomorrow, and there – the third day – we see that the last word is God's.

I remind you again of the words of Charles Rann Kennedy, fictional perhaps, but in keeping with reality: 'I tell you, woman, this dead Son of yours, disfigured, shunned, spat upon, has built a kingdom this day that can never die.' Those who cast their anchor at the cross, and are willing to be patient with the patience of God, will find that evil is destined to break itself upon the facts. The first day and the second day are question marks. But the third day is an exclamation mark!

O God my Father, help me walk through this world, evil though it may be, with the confidence that everything is under Your control. Mystifying though it is to me, I know there is a purpose in everything. Help me hold on to that – always. Amen.

EVERY DAY WITH JESUS

With around half a million readers, this compact bimonthly devotional is one of the most popular daily Bible-reading tools in the world. Be challenged, comforted and encouraged and get practical help with life's challenges while gaining insight into the deeper truths of scripture.

Every Day with Jesus
– bimonthly daily Bible-reading notes
72-page paperback, 120x170mm
Also available:
UK annual subscription (6 issues),
Email subscription
Large-print edition (210x297mm).

JOURNEY THROUGH THE BIBLE AS IT HAPPENED – IN A YEAR OF DAILY READINGS

Read through the entire Bible with 366 daily readings from *The New International Version* (NIV), arranged in chronological order. Beautiful charts, maps, illustrations and diagrams plus daily commentary help you to apply God's Word to your life.

Cover to Cover Complete – NIV Edition
1,600-page hardback, 140x215mm
ISBN: 978-1-85345-804-0

For current prices visit **www.cwr.org.uk/store**
Available online or from Christian bookshops